CEDAR MILL COMM LIBRARY
12505 NW CORNELL RD
PORTLAND, OR 97229
(503) 644-0043

S0-BCO-662

WITHDRAWN
CEDAR MILL & BETHANY LIBRARIES

EVERYDAY **STEM**

HOW ROBOTS WORK

N CHOW-MILLER

Cavendish
Square
New York

Published in 2019 by Cavendish Square Publishing, LLC
243 5th Avenue, Suite 136, New York, NY 10016

Copyright © 2019 by Cavendish Square Publishing, LLC

First Edition

No part of this publication may be reproduced, stored in a retrieval system, or transmitted in any form or by any means—electronic, mechanical, photocopying, recording, or otherwise—without the prior permission of the copyright owner. Request for permission should be addressed to Permissions, Cavendish Square Publishing, 243 5th Avenue, Suite 136, New York, NY 10016. Tel (877) 980-4450; fax (877) 980-4454.

Website: cavendishsq.com

This publication represents the opinions and views of the author based on his or her personal experience, knowledge, and research. The information in this book serves as a general guide only. The author and publisher have used their best efforts in preparing this book and disclaim liability rising directly or indirectly from the use and application of this book.

All websites were available and accurate when this book was sent to press.

Library of Congress Cataloging-in-Publication Data

Names: Chow-Miller, Ian, author.
Title: How robots work / Ian Chow-Miller.
Description: New York : Cavendish Square, 2019. | Series: Everyday STEM |
Includes bibliographical references and index.
Identifiers: LCCN 2017051570 (print) | LCCN 2017058774 (ebook) |
ISBN 9781502637475 (ebook) | ISBN 9781502637444 (library bound) |
ISBN 9781502637451 (pbk.) | ISBN 9781502637468 (6 pack) |
Subjects: LCSH: Robots--Juvenile literature. | Robotics--Juvenile literature.
Classification: LCC TJ211.2 (ebook) | LCC TJ211.2 .C53428 2019 (print) |DDC 629.8/92--dc23
LC record available at https://lccn.loc.gov/2017051570

Editorial Director: David McNamara
Editor: Meghan Lamb
Copy Editor: Nathan Heidelberger
Associate Art Director: Amy Greenan
Designer: Alan Sliwinski/Christina Shults
Production Coordinator: Karol Szymczuk
Photo Research: J8 Media

The photographs in this book are used by permission and through the courtesy of:
Photo credits: Cover Liu Guanguan/China News Service/VCG/Getty Images; p. 4 Kirsty Pargeter/Alamy Stock Photo; p. 6 Aplus/Shutterstock.com; p. 7 Isak55/Shutterstock.com; p. 8 Garry Gay/Photolibrary/Getty Images; p. 10 da Vinci Surgical System; p. 11 Dmitry Kalinovsky/Shutterstock.com; p. 13 © Osada/Seguin/DRASSM; p. 14 RPBaiao/Shutterstock.com; p. 15 Blend Images/Alamy Stock Photo; p. 16 Solarbotics; p. 17 Frank Ramspott/iStockphoto.com; p. 20 Bas Nastassia/Shutterstock.com; p. 21 Imagentle/Shutterstock.com; p. 22 Tatiana Shepeleva/Shutterstock.com; p. 24 Darq/Shutterstock.com; p. 25 Abraksis/Shutterstock.com; p. 26 Patrick Aventurier/Getty Images.

Printed in the United States of America

CONTENTS

These robots are following instructions.

CHAPTER 1
WHAT IS A ROBOT?

When you imagine a robot, what do you see? Do you picture a person made of metal? Do you picture a talking computer? Do you picture a dishwasher, a toaster, or some other tool you might find in your house? There are many different kinds of robots all around us in our daily lives.

Robot or Machine?

A robot is different from a **machine**. A machine is a tool with many parts that work together. A machine is made to do one thing exactly the same way every single time. A robot can be **programmed** to do

A dishwasher can do work for you, but it is a machine, not a robot.

new things in different ways. Let's look at the different parts of this definition closely.

Like machines, robots need power to work. A robot also needs to be programmable. That means you can tell it what to do by pushing a few buttons or writing some **code**. You can program it to carry out new actions. This is what makes a robot different from a machine.

Have you ever watched an adult use a lawn mower? A lawn mower is an example of a machine. If a machine needs help to work, it is not a robot. A lawn mower is not a robot because you have to push it around your yard.

This is a sample of the code that runs robots.

A robot can be programmed to do many different tasks all by itself. Search-and-rescue robots are a good example. They are programmed to go into a building

A search-and-rescue robot could safely search this building.

after an earthquake and find people trapped inside. The search-and-rescue robots do not need any help to find people. They face new changes every time they go into a building. The weather might be rainy one day and sunny on another day. The building might be dark or light inside. There might still be shaking from the earthquake. The search-and-rescue robots are programmed to do different things in different spaces.

A robot runs on electricity. This can come from an electrical plug, a battery, or solar energy (sun power). A fully powered robot will continue to do its job.

Is It a Robot?

Think back to the beginning of this chapter. I asked if you pictured a dishwasher or a toaster when you thought about robots. Could they be robots? Let's think about it.

Are they machines that follow a set of instructions? Yes. Do they do this on their own, without any help? Yes. You just push a button

FAST FACT

The word "robot" comes from a play written in 1920 called *Rossum's Universal Robots*. The play was written in Czech. In that language, the word *robota* means "to be forced to work."

and they start. Can they be programmed? Well, a little bit. You can have dark toast or light toast. You can put your dishwasher through an extra

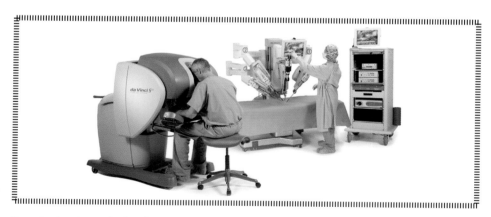

Surgical robots help doctors operate inside a person's body.

rinse cycle. That's about all they can do. Because they cannot do different things, these machines are not really robots.

So, what are robots? There are many different types. There are industrial robots that help build cars or planes. There are surgical robots that can help a doctor fix a person's heart, like the Da Vinci surgery robot.

There are robots that can help you clean the house, like the robotic vacuum called a Roomba. There are educational robots. There are drones, search-and-rescue robots,

A drone is like a programmable airplane.

THE GOOD AND BAD OF ROBOTS

Every technology has good and bad points. Robots are no different. One of the biggest positives about robots is they can do jobs that human beings cannot. For example, a robot can go into a dangerous area, like a building that fell in an earthquake, and search for people. A robot can work on another planet because it does not have to breathe. A robot can do work on the bottom of the ocean floor. Broken buildings, planets, and the ocean floor are all places people would have problems living and working in, but robots would not.

A negative thing about robots is that some people say they take away jobs from humans. For example, a lot of people used to work in factories. Because factories need workers to do things over and over in the same exact

This robot can go deep underwater, where it would be dangerous for people.

manner, they are a great place for robots to work. Robots can work in a factory doing the same thing over and over all day long without getting tired. They can even keep working all night long. If robots can do the work better, faster, and longer, people may not be able to work in factories.

and many, many others. They all have a few things in common. They can be programmed to follow instructions, and they do different kinds of work.

ENGINEERING AND ALGORITHMS

Do you build things? Do you use LEGO or wood blocks? Maybe you have built a pillow fort in the house. All of these require **engineering**. Engineering means putting things together. If you've ever built a fort

This LEGO tower is an example of engineering.

that fell over, then rebuilt it so it doesn't fall down, you have learned about engineering.

Mechanical engineering—or machine engineering—makes a robot strong and stable. Robots use **motors** to move. These motors need power. Electrical engineering is also needed to build a robot. This means you must know how to connect wires from the power (like a battery) to the different parts of the robot.

Do you know how to make a peanut butter and jelly sandwich? I'll bet

Pillow forts are a great way to get started with engineering.

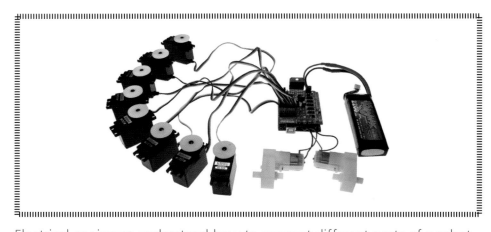

Electrical engineers understand how to connect different parts of a robot together with wires.

you do. There is a long list of steps to finish this task. You take out bread. You take out peanut butter and jelly. You take out a knife. You spread peanut butter and jelly on the bread.

Another word for this long list of steps is an **algorithm**. When a programmer wants to give robots instructions, he or she writes an algorithm. The programmer translates it into code using a computer language the robot understands. Different robots use different computer languages, so the programmer must be very good at writing code.

FAST FACT

Robots will drive into a wall or off a cliff and smash themselves to pieces, even if they use their sensors to see the wall or cliff. Robots need to be told what to do. Driving and seeing is not enough. You must remember to program the robot to stop and go a different direction, or it will crash.

All the parts of the robot must work together for it to be successful.

CHAPTER 2

THE DIFFERENT PARTS OF A ROBOT

Robots are not human, but we can use the human body to help us understand them. A robot has a part called a processor that works like a brain. The processor has sensors that work like our eyes and ears. A processor can also sense many things a human cannot.

Robots have a body that supports and holds everything together. Some robots have parts like arms, legs, and wheels. All of these parts work together to make a robot. Let's see how.

The special sensor on top of this robot helps it to see.

A ROBOT'S BRAIN

A robot does not have a brain that thinks like a human—at least not yet! A programmer fills a part of the robot's brain with codes. These codes tell the robot what to do. They tell the robot how to send out information. And they tell the robot how to gather information.

This part of the robot's brain is called the processor. The processor has many electrical parts. It has places for power to be connected to it. It has places for wires to be connected to sensors and motors.

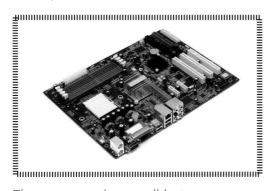

The processor is a small but very important part of a robot.

The processor reads the code a programmer sends to it. Then, it follows the code's instructions. These instructions could be to turn a motor, flash a light, or honk a horn. Whatever the action is,

there must be a part
to carry out that
action. These parts
are called **outputs**
because information
is sent out to them
from the processor.

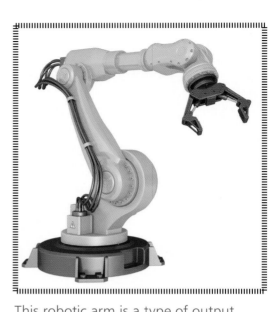

This robotic arm is a type of output.

The most
common type of
output on a robot
is a motor. A motor is a special part of a
machine that provides movement. Electricity
causes a motor to spin around when the code
tells it to. A motor can connect to a wheel for
moving. It can connect to an arm for lifting,
grabbing, or pushing.

NEED HELP? SAY HELLO TO YOUR NEW BEST FRIEND, BAXTER

Have you ever seen a blind person with a seeing-eye dog helping him or her walk down the street? The dogs are very good at stopping at intersections and waiting for the light to turn green. But can the dog tell which bus is the right one? Can a dog tell if a subway train is late or not? No, a dog can't do these things. But a robot can. Scientists are developing a robot called Baxter whose job will be to help blind people get around a city. Baxter can use its computer brain (processor) to get information about which bus is coming. It can find out if a train is late or a store is closed. Baxter can also stop at a busy road or a red light like a seeing-eye dog. As a matter of fact, the only thing that Baxter can't do is lick your face and slobber on you. At least not yet.

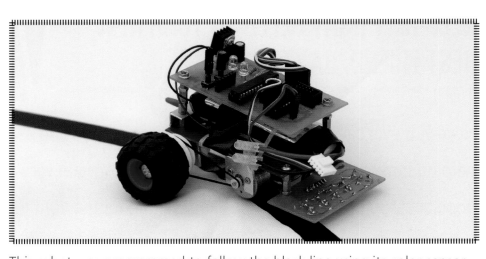

This robot was programmed to follow the black line using its color sensor.

The opposite of outputs are **inputs**. In robotics, the inputs are called sensors. Sensors take in information. Then, they send the information to the processor. The processor makes decisions.

There are many types of sensors in a robot. Some sensor types are color, light, sound, and temperature. They are similar to senses humans have, like the ability to see, hear, and feel.

Let's again compare a robot to the human body. The sensors are like eyes and ears. The

This sensor tells how close an object is.

processor is like a brain. The motors are like joints connected to robot arms or legs.

FAST FACT

The fastest running robot is called WildCat. It has four legs and gallops like a horse. It can run at a top speed of 20 miles per hour (32 kilometers per hour), faster than a human being!

A Robot's Body

Let's picture the body of the robot. The body of a robot may not look like a human body, but it does the same things. The body holds the whole robot together. It connects the brain to all the other parts. The body of a robot can be made out of different materials, like plastic or metal.

A robot that looks like a person is called a "humanoid" robot.

Robots are everywhere. They are in factories, hospitals, homes, schools, the army, and many other places. If you are going to understand the world around you as you grow up, you will have to know a little bit about robots. Remember, even if a robot looks like a person, it doesn't think or feel like a human being. However, robots can be programmed to do the same things as humans, and so much more.

FAST FACT

Robots have been built that can solve a Rubik's Cube in less than one second! The fastest human has done it in 4.69 seconds, but scientists have built a robot that can solve one in 0.637 seconds. Now that's fast!

TECHNOLOGY TIMELINE

1921   The word "robot" is used in a play to mean "forced work."

1954   The first programmable robot, Unimate, is developed by George Devol.

1969   Victor Scheinman creates the Stanford Arm, which is the first successful electrically powered, computer-controlled robot arm.

2002   The Roomba, a robotic vacuum, is introduced.

2012   Paralyzed patients use their mind to control a robotic arm.

algorithm A step-by-step method for solving a problem.

code A set of instructions written in language a robot can understand; "code" can refer to part of a larger program or to the entire program itself.

engineering A branch of science concerned with building machines, buildings, robots, and other structures.

input When information is put into a computer or robot.

machine An item made of different parts that uses power to perform a task repeatedly.

motor A machine that uses electricity.

output Information that is sent out from a robot's processor to motors, lights, or other parts.

program To write an algorithm in language a robot can read.

FIND OUT MORE

BOOKS

O'Hearn, Michael. *Amazing Space Robots:* Capstone
Press, 2013.

Stewart, Melissa. *Robots.* Washington, DC: National
Geographic Society, 2014.

WEBSITES

Galileo Education Network: Robotics

http://www.galileo.org/robotics/intro.html

Razor Robotics

https://www.razorrobotics.com

INDEX

Page numbers in **boldface** are illustrations.

ABOUT THE AUTHOR

Ian Chow-Miller is a robotics and engineering middle-school teacher. He is a member of the LEGO Education Advisory Panel and is a constant contributor to Tufts University's LEGO Engineering website. Ian coaches robotics and soccer teams after school. He is married to an awesome wife and has two great sons who are budding artists and engineers.